I0177408

I'm Worth Loving!
Here's Why.

by

DR. GILDA CARLE

Published in New York by
InterChange Communications Training, Inc.

Copyright © 2016 InterChange Communications
Training, Inc.

Gilda-Gram® is a registered trademark owned by
InterChange Communications Training, Inc.

Disclaimer: Private individuals depicted throughout this
book are composites. To protect privacy interests, all
names and identifying details have been changed, and
emails have been adapted or paraphrased.

All rights reserved under international and
Pan-American Copyright Conventions. No part of this
publication may be reproduced, stored in a retrieval
system or transmitted, in any form or by any means,
electronic, mechanical, photocopying, recording or
otherwise, without the prior permission of the copyright
holder.

ISBN-13: 978-1-881829-10-2

Library of Congress Control Number: 2015904246

Printed in the United States

For more information visit
www.DrGilda.com

ACKNOWLEDGMENTS

Thank you to all who have so generously contributed your true stories to help others who are reading this book. Without your giving, there would be less healthful living!
--Dr. Gilda

Gilda-Gram®
The secret to attracting healthy love
is to believe
YOU'RE WORTH LOVING!

CONTENTS

***

CHAPTER 1
WHAT IS YOUR WORTH?

If you were asked to name a figure describing what you are worth, what dollar amount would you assign yourself? Would you say you're worth $1 million? More? Less? When I was teaching kids in the inner city in the New York public schools, I distributed a poster to my students that said, "I know I'm somebody, 'cause God don't make no junk." The kids and their parents clamored for numerous copies to hang in their homes and put in their notebooks. The poster served as a reminder that, despite their impoverished living conditions, these kids needed to constantly be reminded to value themselves.

Expressing your self-worth is good for your emotional, as well as your physical, health, but most people don't ordinarily take stock in these attributes. Consequently, they suffer from low self-esteem and the dysfunctional relationships that follow low self-esteem.

Gilda-Gram®
Valuing your worth determines how you navigate the world.

Therefore, first determining your personal value

is the most important action you can take for finding love. And it actually begins with assigning yourself real value in terms of a dollar-and-cents figure! At first glance, giving yourself a numeric value may seem strange and superficial. But your physiological components really can be assessed.

According to the American Chemical Society, if you were to appraise the value of the elements in the body, the value of the elements in your body, the price tag would come to a mere $1.25! However, when these chemicals operate *together*, their unique interaction produces hormones, proteins, and nucleic acids that bump up your true worth to nearly $8 million! (To think we once revered the less costly Six Million Dollar Man!) How many people know enough to strut their stuff because it's worth $8 million?

Each time I receive an email from someone describing a problem they're having, it saddens me to detect feelings of self-doubt at the heart of the issue. Unfortunately, after years of assessing and counseling relationship problems from the bedroom to the boardroom, I have found that the basis of most of these problems lies in a person's lack of appreciation for who he or she really is. Let me show you specifically what I mean. See if you can figure out the underlying issue in the following email I received:

Dear Dr. Gilda,

I am a 32-year-old woman who just left a 3-year relationship. I was married once for a very short time.

As I look back, I recognize that my ex-boyfriend was just a little nicer than my ex-husband. Now I see similarities between the two that should have been red flags, but which I missed. In both relationships, I was the "giver." In the end, both men told me, "You are the best thing that ever happened to me. I just can't give you what you need." It leaves me feeling as though I did something wrong.

My ex-boyfriend, Todd, was always unsure about what type of commitment he could offer me. I ignored it when he continued to tell me that. I just went on with our lives and pretended those issues were not there. We relocated to another city for his job. I totally turned my life around to be with him and his two small children.

When we relocated, we had already been together for about a year. We took full custody of his boys and settled in to our little family life. I naturally took on the role of stepmom. It was a struggle for me, since I don't have children of my own.

Todd and I seemed to be in love, or so I thought. I did the household chores and I also supported everyone emotionally. I even quit my new job to be a stay-at-home mommy. I realize now that I totally lost myself in this arrangement.

Todd was very wishy-washy towards me. One day I would feel as if he was deeply in love with me, but the next day I would wake up and be anxious all day, worrying that he would end our relationship. Well, my

3

worst fear came true after 2 years. Todd said he wasn't sure he ever wanted to get remarried or have any more children. I moved back home.

After I settled in again, I got a great job and tried to move forward with my life. But my heart was still with Todd and the boys. After about a month, he called and said the words every girl dreams of: "My life is so much better when you are in it. I want to get married and have a child with you." I was so excited that, without question, I immediately quit my job again and headed back to them. I thought that he finally realized that we should be permanently together, and I was filled with joy.

Things were great for about a month. Then we slipped back into our former routine. Todd was an alcoholic and would leave me home with his kids to go out to the bar. He would get mad at me for getting upset with him. That's when I realized this was not healthy. He would treat me as though I was the best thing and the worst thing that ever happened to him.

Three months after I moved back to them, I ended up packing and leaving again. He was back to the same old thing, telling me he still wasn't sure if he wanted to get married and have a child. He told me he was sorry, but I knew there was more to it than that. I realize now that he is not capable of having a healthy relationship.

I have been gone for one month and Todd is

already living with another woman. Mutual friends call her a "trashy lady." They met the week after I left. She brought both her children to live with Todd and his boys. I am in shock. How can he go from one person to the next so quickly? How can he subject his children to another woman? I realize their relationship is probably far from perfect. From what I hear, she assists him in his drinking and drugging. He tells friends, "I am so in love." His friends tell him he is crazy and refuse to hang out with him as long as she is in the picture.

Even though I know theirs is probably not a healthy relationship, I am still hurt. I feel as though everything he told me is a lie. He is a lie. For the most part, I am happy to be out of the relationship. But the other part of me is so hurt that he can go from one to the other after all I did for him and all I gave up for him. Doesn't he realize this?

Dr. Gilda, what did I do wrong? How do I get over these feelings and move on the way he did? I have gone out on a few dates, but I don't want anything serious for now. Please help me.
Macy

Dear Macy,

Before we discuss what really happened in your relationship, answer this question: How much do you believe you are worth? Your response to this question sets you up to determine who you choose as a partner, why you choose him, and how you will relate as the romance progresses.

From all you've said, you clearly don't believe you're worth enough! By your own admission, you placed your needs on the back burner in favor of your boyfriend's. As a result, your own needs, the crux of what guides you day-to-day, simply fell off the stove. When you abandoned your notion of protecting yourself, and you elevated your boyfriend's needs above your own, you abandoned your personal sense of worth. Now let's examine why this happened.

HE: A Dependent Personality. Todd is addicted to alcohol and drugs. While you admit to his alcohol addiction, it was only when discussing the other woman that you casually mentioned the existence of drugs. Addictions to substances such as these reflect a dependent personality type. To prove my point, the moment you left Todd, his dependency needs immediately switched from you to another woman. Girlfriend, this guy didn't even miss a beat before he became enmeshed again! A dependent personality cannot be alone without his drug of choice. And if one drug isn't enough, he'll reach for others, as well.

Dependent personality types usually choose an array of feel-good drugs so they'll never falter. Todd chose drugs, alcohol, AND SAVIORS. So however he derives his fix, from whoever is around, any likely candidate, person, or substance will do the trick. To this guy, one woman taking care of him and his sons is as good as another.

I know Todd's dependence is tough for you to

admit. Everyone in a relationship with someone she loves would like to think of herself as "special." However, now you must accept the fact that Todd needs a constant caretaker, and you were a convenient, generous, and available target.

If you had had, and if you maintained, a sense of self-worth, you would never have dismissed your own needs. Further, no one would have been able to take advantage of your good nature as Todd had. But, as it stood, you willingly shed your sense of self in favor of your lover and his sons. As a result, you were perfect to become Todd' prey. Look at all the things you gave up because you were needy for love.

<u>Gilda-Gram®</u>
Never settle for anyone just to have someone.

<u>YOU: A Needy Personality</u>. *Macy, you were so anxious to have a marriage and family, you accepted Todd and the boys to fill your void, unconditionally, without creating boundaries. All relationships need boundaries, particularly when more than two people are involved. While you were enacting your role as super-lover and super-mom, you admit that you ignored Todd's inability to commit to you. If you had valued your own worth, you would never have been attracted to Todd or anyone like him.*

Even if you were, at some point early on attracted to this guy, you would have heard what he was really trying to tell you, and you'd have evacuated his premises for greener pastures. But you heard what you wanted to hear, and you fantasized that by being a great mate, you would get him over his fears. In other words, you tried to be the perfect savior so he would remain with you.

Sure, occasionally, to keep you intact in your caretaking role, Todd mouthed the loving words you longed to hear. But his promises kept changing, and he couldn't stick to being devoted. Still, you chose to ignore the signs, betting that eventually he would come around.

THE THIRD PARTY: Who Cares? *What difference does it make about the kind of relationship Todd has with the woman who replaced you? Who cares how trashy she is? Who cares about her own two children who she added to his household? Her existence is not your concern. Of course it hurts to think you've been replaced, and so quickly and easily! Anyone in that situation would similarly feel your pain. Unfortunately, a dependent man, as Todd is, would just rationalize that he has simply moved on. Now that you're away from him physically, it's time for you to exit emotionally. Of course it will take time.*

Give yourself a time limit to feel depressed and angry, but on the date you've circled on your calendar, call a halt to all bad feelings over the situation. Whenever you slip back into those feelings, get yourself to snap out of it by considering all you learned. Eventually, you'll be able to add pleasure to your life with someone or something far more worthy of your output.

What you must especially do now is to take comfort in the fact that no relationship, not one for Todd, nor one for you, can possibly work out until each of you has done some alone-time thinking and processing. His problems are his problems. But as for you, it's imperative to discover what really happened in this romance and why. Since Todd's too afraid to be alone, I doubt if he will ever do the emotional probing that he must, but as I said, that's his problem.

Now is the time for you to explore the past as it really was, so that you will not repeat these behaviors in the future. Once you learn the true lessons that came with this situation, you will have grown a lot and you will have prepared yourself for a healthier union in the future.

Macy, please understand that your main objective now is to learn to value yourself. Because you didn't value your worth at the start of this relationship, you accepted what I call "Less-Than Treatment" from a man who was not capable of giving you what you wanted. You tried to dismiss the reality that stared you in the face. You lived with him, you left him, you returned . . . all in the hope that this guy would change. As I tell every woman, the only male you will ever change is the one you're in charge of when he's in diapers!

The saddest part of all is that you gave up jobs you adored, along with your soul, just to be loved. In

9

the end, not only didn't you receive the love you set out to get, but while you were taking care of Todd and his boys, you derailed an enjoyable career path for yourself.

When you give to the point of your own exhaustion, it's called "overfunctioning." Girl, there's only so much energy and time that any of us have!
Dr. Gilda

Gilda-Gram®
When you overfunction for a partner, you underfunction for yourself.

Simply, the way to assess someone's love for you is to determine whether you are the most important person in your lover's life.

Some people think they are doing their partners a favor by overfunctioning for them. So they become a lover's caretaker, believing, at least subconsciously, that their partner will hold onto them, since now he is depending on the benefits he's deriving. That's a big miscalculation!

Gilda-Gram®
Your value is NOT about what you DO; it's about who you ARE.

People who haven't yet figured this out need to get a new definition of "selfish." The opposite of selfish is selfLESS. If you attempt to have a relationship based on *less* of yourself, you set yourself up to bore your partner. Yuk! Who wants to be with a shadow of a person?

As self-serving as it may appear, keep in mind that the first word of the all-too-often-used phrase, "I love you," is "I," and it comes with a Capital. If you are unwilling to enunciate your Capital I, you are on the road to abdicating your power, and passing it along to someone less worthy than you.

Nobody in the world can love you or care for you as well as YOU can love and care for yourself. Nobody in the world can know your greatest desires as well as you can. Nobody in the world will be there for you the way you will be.

So if YOU are not the one marketing your own worth, how will anyone else be able to do it for you? They can't. And while the famous Jerry McGuire movie made us all cry when the main character said to the woman he had regrettably left, "You complete me," the truth is that NOBODY can complete you but you. Sorry!

In another note to Macy, I said,

Ask yourself whether your overfunctioning for this guy was being fair to you. I bet you never even considered what was in YOUR best interests. Certainly, Todd didn't look out for your needs. In a healthy relationship, when you value yourself, you don't need to desperately seek your value from your mate. When you know you're worth it, you will attract a partner who feels secure about himself. Two worthy people don't require one to babysit the other. When you're dealing with two worthy people, each can bring to the union a mature and nurturing perspective that helps the relationship flourish.

Coming to grips with all that went on and the hurt you feel now will naturally take time. You need this time to gain insight about the past and to appreciate your value. Believe it or not, the more value you place on yourself, the sooner you will accept that you were with a man who didn't honor and embrace all you brought to the table. As for what you can do this very second, be grateful Todd is out of your life! If you do the work I'm suggesting you do, you will attract a much more appropriate partner.
Dr. Gilda

Where did women ever get the notion that it is their responsibility to save their guys? Since I have a number of books for teens on the market, I also hear from young girls whose "disease to please" puts their own needs on hold. Does this next email sound like a teen you know?

Dear Dr. Gilda,

Okay, like any other story, this starts with a guy. A very handsome and sweet guy. He's one of the cutest guys in our high school. We've been friends since Christmas and we've hung out every couple of weekends. Now my dilemma is that he just doesn't see himself as cute or good-looking. He has such low self-esteem that I just don't know how to help him out. It makes me really

depressed because he's down in the dumps so often. I would tell him that I care about him, but I've been hurt enough in my life and I don't want to get hurt again. I try to encourage him, but it doesn't even make a dent. Do you have any suggestions on how I could help him feel better?
Paula

Hey, Paula,

*Let's examine what you're really saying here. You write, "Now my dilemma is that he just doesn't see himself as cute or good-looking." For starters, THIS IS NOT **YOUR** DILEMMA. You go on, "It makes me really depressed because he's down in the dumps so often." Why are YOU getting depressed over HIS low self-esteem? At last, you write, "I try to encourage him, but it doesn't even make a dent." Who made you this guy's teacher, healer, social worker, and SAVIOR? If it doesn't even make a dent, as you say, then this guy is probably not interested in your assistance.*

The question really is NOT "How can I help this guy?," but instead, "Why do I even want a guy who needs such an overhaul?" With all the effort you've already put into this attempt at a relationship, you should take your effort and invest it in yourself. At least, as you grow and develop, you'll appreciate your own achievements. Meanwhile, if you really want to make a difference in people's lives, why not volunteer at a hospital for sick children or at an animal shelter? At least then, your efforts will not be in vain.
Dr. Gilda

While Paula is only a high school student, there are too many grown women who suffer from the same "dilemma" of the disease to please. This malady places women's needs as secondary to those of the man, or others, they love. In the end, the recipients of their kindness take them for granted, lose respect for them, and eventually toss them aside for someone more challenging.

Visiting Los Angeles to film my last movie, I had lunch with a friend who has a very high-level job in the entertainment business. She brought along a friend of hers who was also doing well. My friend talked about working too hard, often finding that assignments delegated to some of her subordinates ended up recycled onto her desk. She confided that she wanted to always be sure that the "t's" were crossed and the "i's" were dotted, since she is responsible for the bottom line. What's more, she revealed that she also wants everyone to like her.

The other woman had an entirely different issue. She said she always wanted to write, and she asked me loads of questions about some of my own publications. But she shared that she was having difficulty submitting manuscripts to publishers because she feared rejection.

Both women, whose issues were very different, were suffering from the disease to please. My friend took on her staff's burdens so she would be liked. Her friend feared taking on any burdens at all in an effort not to be rejected. The disease to please strikes teens and adults alike, but the disturbing fact is that it is predominantly a female issue. Unfortunately, most women *still* need to learn this:

Gilda-Gram®
I am the person who is most important to please.

This **Gilda-Gram®** is especially applicable when people fall in love. To avoid the consequences of this ailment, then, should women stop trying to please a partner, and instead play hard to get? Never! I'd never suggest that women *play* any game. If a woman finds herself more concerned, and even depressed, over her guy's problems than she is over her own, that's her cue to get a life. Actually, when she has a rich and exciting life herself, her guy will have to overcome the obstacles of capturing her heart. And that's when he'll find her most appealing. The principle is based on the most basic psychology:

Gilda-Gram®
People value most what they work hardest to get.

This **Gilda-Gram®** explains why we find the most difficult "bad boys" to be the most attractive. It also explains the reason that guys we're not interested in pursue us the hardest.

What does all this tell us? Simply, that we're most attractive to potential suitors and friends when we're most involved in what we love. Do you follow that formula, or do you lose yourself in your love mate as soon as you connect?

Success in love is totally dependent on how you value your worth. Take the quiz, "Do I Feel Worthy?" below and determine how you assess your value. Beside each statement, write True or False, as it applies to you. Then calculate the number of your True scores at the bottom of the quiz.

Do I Feel Worthy?

____1. I believe I'm responsible for my own happiness.

____2. I surround myself with confident people.

____3. I look forward to work each day.

____4. I make sure to schedule time for the hobbies I love.

____5. I would rate myself as positive and confident.

____6. I handle life's challenges rather than become depressed by them.

____7. I am committed to my goals, but I can also take myself lightly.

____8. I feel comfortable asking for things I need.

____9. I make the effort to take care of my emotional and financial health.

____10. I feel comfortable with my looks and body.

Scoring Key:

8+ Trues: Your self-worth is high. Congratulations!
0 - 7 Trues: Your self-worth needs improvement. Have

faith in yourself and follow the steps in this book. While you're learning more about yourself, take a long, hard look at the people you have been attracting into your life.

Gilda-Gram®

We attract NOT whom we want, but WHO WE ARE.

Identifying whom you are attracting will tell you volumes about yourself—as though you're peering into a mirror. Once you recognize your own part in the partners you're drawing to you, you will have the power to make much healthier changes!

CHAPTER 2
THE KEY TO YOUR VALUE

I have seen people pull the wool over their own eyes, and continue engaging in behavior that's harmful to them. But when they therapeutically commit their feelings to writing—in a journal, an email to themselves, or through a self-assessment quiz, they get to read the things they'd rather not face. It is then that they become a third, impartial party. And becoming the reader, instead of the victim, allows them to readily see whether they're giving up their power—the most crucial beginning point of any relationship.

Gilda-Gram®
When a person gives up her power to her partner, she becomes his dependent.

Without power, we become dependent on our partner to love us. This could be dangerous, because our dependence is contingent on HIS desires and needs. As much as we'd like to enjoy security with this person, what we actually derive instead is insecurity. And this goes for both men and women. Men run from relationships when they think they are being controlled, or when they think their partner is eroding their power.

Macy gave up her power to Todd. If we were to visualize her on a seesaw with Todd and his sons, the guys would be securely seated on the ground, while she would be hanging in mid-air, her arms flailing, pleading with her lover to let her down and love her.

Without personal power, Macy can't push the seesaw down by herself. Instead, she whines about what she did wrong. Yes, unfortunately, it's usually the woman who thinks she did something wrong to cause the relationship to disintegrate. Women consider themselves the "relationship police." Remember all the relationship pruning Macy did at home, while Todd was out on the town, drinking and drugging. Also keep in mind that to do her household chores and mothering, she was certainly able to draw from personal power she did have. But when it came to *caring for herself*, her power had disappeared.

Macy was in deep pain, as anyone would be at the end of such an intense roller coaster ride. Yet this breakup was the best thing that could have happened to her. Now her sole job would be to spend her time alone, trying to recognize why she choose to become involved with such a needy guy. This would be her chance to finally take responsibility for her own part in the merger.

Most people neglect this most important ingredient of relationship survival, which I name "personal responsibility." As a result, as soon as they're out of one bad relationship, they go on to choose partners who are similar, or even identical, to those they just left. As they find themselves enmeshed in one dysfunctional relationship after another, they can't understand why. One woman innocently asked me if she was wearing a T-shirt inscribed with "Kick Me!" It's happened to me, and it's probably happened to you, where we continued to form relationships similar to previous bad ones. Until we're 100% committed to strip emotionally bare, and admit our role in our love meltdown, there is no hope of moving forward.

Read the following story, and determine who was responsible for the plight of this one very beautiful, but confused princess.

Once upon a time, there lived a beautiful princess. Just as fairy tales go, she married the prince of her dreams and lived in a large and luxurious penthouse. Every evening after work, the prince and princess attended the most extravagant parties at the finest palaces, and their friends believed they formed the perfect pair. However, as time went on, the princess was growing bored with just sitting around her digs all day while her prince went off to expand his fortune. When a handsome bad-boy artist came upon her in the lush palace gardens, he was quickly able to seduce her and carry her off to his barren studio in a raunchy part of town. However, after just one day of dalliance, the artist decided the princess had lost her luster. As quickly as when he had arrived, he abandoned her, without a care.

The princess tried desperately to return to her

posh palace, but there was no transportation, and a turbulent storm was beginning to brew. As she walked aimlessly through the barren forest, she found a wise evangelist from whom she sought help. After hearing her story, the evangelist was appalled by the princess's reckless behavior, and he refused to give her any assistance.

She next stumbled upon an investor from whom she also begged for mercy. But mercenary as he was, he demanded a hefty fee for his troubles. Since the princess had no money with her, the investor also refused her pleas for help.

Finally, the princess had no choice but to continue to attempt the trip home by herself. When she was almost at her destination, the storm became so fierce, it devoured her before she could return.

I ask you, the reader, who do you think is responsible for the demise of this princess? Most people agree that the onus of blame should fall on the princess herself. When taken as a make-believe fairy tale, it's easy to see she's responsible for her acts of stupidity and/or evil. But we live in a society that screams, "Don't blame me," a society in which, when expectations are not met, pointing fingers at everyone but ourselves is a popular sport.

Remember how Macy rationalized her breakup with Todd. Instead of admitting her leanings toward loser lovers, she blandly concluded that it was Todd who was "not capable of having a healthy relationship."

What would it take for Macy to recognize that Todd did not hold her captive, bound and gagged, to make her remain with him?

Sadly, as much as we'd like to deny it,

Gilda-Gram®
We attract not whom we want, but who we ARE.

Although it had been in the past, now during her alone time, it was necessary for Macy to examine her brief marriage before Todd appeared in her life. She needed to determine what it really meant, and why it didn't last. She then had to admit that for her next go-around, this time with Todd, she choose an addict. Why? She needed to finally understand what this said about her inability, her disinterest, or her poor perception in selecting a worthy partner.

Gilda-Gram®
Whichever partner we choose says more about US than it says about our partner.

Perhaps Macy needed to feel needed by an underachieving man to pump up her feelings of self-importance. To make herself feel worthy, perhaps Macy needed to derive credit for saving a floundering family from ruin. Obviously, both her husband and Todd, and probably, others she did not mention to me, were as needy as she was.

Whatever her motives for getting involved with

these men, she always ended up as a disappointed woman. But now she was being awarded the gift of time to discover the whys of her past. As a result of her newfound insight, she would become wiser for her future.

Gilda-Gram®
Our test is always whether we're willing to accept how we contributed to each relationship fiasco.

Michelle had been single for two years after her last boyfriend broke up with her. She was interested in meeting someone new, but she was a bit shy to pursue the singles market. She avoided singles bars and she loathed blind dates. Many of her friends had had some good experiences on the Internet, but she was skeptical about promoting herself that way. Her girlfriend, Clara, was an active online dater, which led her to enjoy dates almost every night of the week. One of the men Clara came across seemed nice, but didn't appear to be her type. So Clara sent his photo and bio to Michelle to see if she would like to meet him.

While Michelle was shy, she still maintained high standards about whom she would date. Actually, since her previous relationship had ended, she had a few dates during the two-year span, dating at least ten different guys. Although none of them became a love connection, they were all pleasant and nice.

With interest, she did read the profile Michelle sent to her. One of the things that she most noticed was that this man described his involvement in the advertising business, which he couldn't stand, and freely talked about desperately looking to change careers. Although his photo was handsome enough, this guy's disappointment in his work turned Michelle off. When she told that to Clara, Clara asked, "What do you care whether this guy loves his work or not?" Michelle told her that it made a big difference to her. "If someone is not in love with his life, he would not be able to love a partner," Michelle answered. (She and I had been having steady Skype sessions for two months by then!) Michelle told Clara she would not be interested in the opportunity of even emailing this guy.

Do you think Michelle was right? You bet she was! In a very short time, she had learned her lessons well.

Gilda-Gram®
To be ready for love, you must first love your life.

Discovering whether someone loves his life is quick and easy. If your potential partner is constantly changing jobs, changing living quarters, changing his mind about what is important to him, or is in a continuous state of flux in general, ask him why. Listen carefully, not only for the responses he gives you, but also for the words and feelings he omits. When I asked one eligible bachelor why he constantly travels around the world, he candidly replied, "A moving target can never get hit." His reputation as being a commitment-phoebe was accurate—and he knew it.

Gilda-Gram®
Someone on the move in life will be someone on the move in love.

Is your partner emotionally "settled"? When a person is not, it's a sign he's struggling to find himself. If that's the case, his main objective is his own survival, rather than finding love. It's a simple equation of having only so much time and energy. Yet, I hear from tons of women who want to change their men from the way they find them, and *make them* ready. Duh! How can anyone make anyone else ready for love?

Gilda-Gram®
No one can save another person.

If you've been trying to save someone else, give it up. It's time to turn the page, and save yourself!

Dear Dr. Gilda,

I am in search of a wonderful man who will treat me great. I have come across many good guys, but if it weren't for bad luck, I'd have no luck at all. Help me please!!
Suzie

Dear Suzie,

I'm not in the matchmaking business, so I can't find you that "wonderful man" you're seeking. But YOU can find him yourself! However, if you're blaming "bad luck" for your poor track record in love, you're not allowing yourself to be accountable for whomever you've been attracting.

Look carefully at various patterns that have continued cropping up. For example, do you continue to choose men who are geographically undesirable? Do you routinely run to guys who are attached to someone else? Do you continue to desire men from different social circles you have no access to? Do you periodically have crushes on people who are unattainable?

Unearth the patterns that have not been serving you. Yes, we all are guilty of doing things that bring down our lives. Unearthing these patterns may take you a while to figure out. But write them down over the course of many days. When you have finished this exercise, you will be able to redirect your tastes to more appropriate men. Do I dare wish you good "luck?" ☺ Dr. Gilda

CHAPTER 3
DO YOU ATTRACT WORTHY PARTNERS?

What PATTERNS, yes, PATTERNS, have you been following to select a partner? If you're like most people, you are probably unaware of any personal patterns at all. Take "Your Previous Partner Assessment" and see what you discover.

Your Previous Partner Assessment

1. List the names of the last three people you were involved with.

2. Next to each name, determine which of the following categories into which each partner fell:

   a) <u>Propeller</u>: someone who motivates you to succeed above and beyond your dreams.

   b) <u>Maintainer</u>: someone who happily accepts you as you are, wherever that may be.

   c) <u>Drainer</u>: someone who emotionally drains your desire and motivation to succeed.

3. Next to each name, write the reason the relationship broke up.

4. If you're involved with someone now, classify him or her as a Propeller, Maintainer, or Drainer.

5. How would you categorize *yourself* in this relationship with your current partner: Propeller, Maintainer, or Drainer?

Scoring Key:

After examining your responses, did you find a PATTERN of behaviors? For example, do you tend to choose Propellers who exhaust you, or Drainers who put you down? Do you act as a Propeller for your partners? Do you help them Maintain their life style? This assessment gives you insight into your behaviors, instead of traditionally examining those of your partners.

Author and metaphysical counselor, Carolyn Myss, classifies personalities into four distinct categories she names "archetypes." They are "the victim," "the child," "the saboteur," and "the prostitute." Each type symbolizes life's challenges. Each also represents how we make our choices to survive.

Myss's "victim" is the passive complainer who plays off others' pity. The "child" is mired in irresponsibility and needs to grow up. The "saboteur" is fearful, self-deprecating, and self-destructive, often undermining not just himself, but others, as well. The "prostitute," which, according to this author's definition, has nothing to do with sex, sells or negotiates his integrity for either survival or financial gain.

Each personality type challenges our ability to maintain our power. Each pushes us to reveal our vulnerability beyond our comfort zone. All represent obstacles in our path to love, and how we choose to overcome them determines who we are, and how successful our relationships will be.

Based on Myss's categories, Macy was the victim because she was willing to dismiss her own needs, yet complain about being hurt after she willingly gave away her power. But she was also the prostitute because she was willing to barter her sense of self in exchange for love. Not surprisingly, her relationship with Todd worked well because he was the needy child who grabbed whatever nourishment he could get. But he was also the saboteur because once his emotional sustenance had been satiated, just like a child, he "killed the goose that laid the golden egg." Together the pair navigated a tumultuous love affair that had all the earmarks for predicting derailment. Todd never took responsibility for his actions, but neither did Macy. However, on a much more positive note, I'm betting that Macy will succeed in love after all, because it was she who reached out to me for help.

Gilda-Gram®
Only when we're vulnerable are we willing to examine our pain.

As much as it hurts, pain serves a very important role in our lives. No one wakes up in the morning with a wonderful and happy lifestyle, and suddenly decides to change it. I'm sure that Macy was at last ready to take responsibility for all the men she attracted in the past who did her harm. That would require courage, which most people find ONLY after they've reached rock bottom.

Are you ready to revamp the "comfort" of what you think you have, as difficult as it may be, for the huge question mark that accompanies the unknown? If you are, the one technique I suggest that promises lasting love is what I call "I Count Caring." It requires a Capital "I" and a strong sense of who you are, and extends to loving your partner because you already know how to love yourself.

When you follow the "I Count Caring" philosophy, you never give your power away, you always accept emotional accountability for your end of the relationship bargain, and you disclose yourself so your partner feels comfortable about disclosing his feelings, too. Without even realizing it, "I Count Caring" insures that you receive great treatment from your partner because you have set into motion a basis for respect.

These days, reality TV is omnipresent, especially for relationship issues. But as much as they are promoted as being "realistic," there's a lot of posturing that is deliberately done for the cameras. If viewers try to model their own relationships after what they see on the small screen, they're likely to be disappointed.

However, reality shows do serve a positive

purpose in that they raise crucial issues we must deal with before we become involved in real relationships. For example, what uniquely motivates us to find a partner? How emotionally available are we? Are looks or the size of a partner's wallet more important to us than other things?

If people probed these questions before they got married, perhaps the divorce rate would go down. One of my goals is to get people to face reality before it's too late. Monica is one such person. She has hidden from the truth for three long years of her relationship, and still, she continues to cover her eyes. Yet, if she didn't believe in her gut that something was not right, she would not have sent me this email:

Dear Dr. Gilda,

I have been with my man for 3 years. We love each other, we don't have a bad relationship, and the only flaw in it really is the Internet. I recently found a letter he sent to a woman online, saying he wanted to meet her. He gave her another email address so she can contact him.

So far she has not emailed him back. What should I do? I love him dearly, and we always talk about getting married. He said he wants me to be the mother of his kids. Does he love me or is he just having fun? But is his giving this woman a separate email address cheating in the full sense of the word?
Monica

Dear Monica,

    Okay, girlfriend, it's time to get real. For starters,

Gilda-Gram®
Dump the fairy tale mentality.

    You're not Cinderella, Prince Charming will never come to rescue you, and there's no Fairy Godmother to provide you with a happy life! Sorry for the reality check!! Part of your reality training is to ask yourself how you can say that this is a terrific relationship except for the Internet. Get real in accepting that your boyfriend is interested in meeting another woman, that he uses a separate email address to continue his correspondence, and that while he probably IS having fun with you, it is certainly not "fun" for you when your emotions, and your relationship, are at stake.

    I don't care how much this guy swears that he wants to get married and make you the mother of his kids. Talk is cheap, and your guy's talk is cheaper than you're willing to believe! Further, he's cheapening the relationship the two of you share by bringing someone else into the picture. I'm sorry to have to tell you that this IS cheating in the full sense of the word. And I pity the other woman who knows nothing about you and the promises you're getting from this two-timer.

    Now let's get more real. How do you know about what your guy is doing on the Internet? Have you been snooping into his email? Just think about what a horrible marriage you would have with a husband who is sneaking around and a wife who is snooping around. Is this what you want to bring children into the world to see?

It's time to finally believe you're worth more than this. Believe you deserve the whole enchilada instead of a few tiny crumbs. Carry yourself with pride and waltz right out of this disrespectful arrangement.

If you were to finally display your power, your guy wouldn't know what hit him. Before you commit to a life with any guy, you'd better be certain he's totally yours. Otherwise, permanently ship out. If you assure yourself that you deserve better, that's exactly what you'll attract.
Dr. Gilda

CHAPTER 4
GETTING THE WHOLE ENCHILADA

Like Monica, I hear from too many people who actually feel they don't deserve a decent partner. So instead, they put up with Less-Than Treatment. No rationalization that the Monicas of the world could ever conjure up would support the way their partners treat them. Yet, they're willing to blame it on boys being boys and having fun. The real deal is that:

Gilda-Gram®
People who feel worthy never accept Less-Than Treatment.

For those who refuse to accept Less-Than Treatment, even if they occasionally slip and find themselves with a put-down partner, as soon as they recognize his behavior for what it truly is, they dart for the door. If this is such a simple rule to follow, why are people so adamant to hold on?

Dear Dr. Gilda,

Harry and I are friends. I moved in next door to him almost two years ago (I have since moved away). He has a live-in girlfriend, Mary. From the beginning,

Mary would complain to me about Harry's shortcomings. Observing their interactions, I advised Mary that she did not have it too bad. She is living in a nice house for free, Harry devotedly comes home to her every night, he gives her a kiss, and he hangs around when he is not playing sports. (I should honestly tell you that I had an instant attraction to Harry from the start, but dismissed it because of his relationship with Mary.)

One summer, a rainstorm had inundated my house and Harry was kind enough to put in a bypass drainage system that kept the water from going into the basement. As he was shoveling the dirt, he suddenly stopped and said, "I just can't take it anymore with Mary." From what each of them independently tells me, neither even likes the other. I counsel both of them, attempting to help them to get along. Our custom was to eat dinner together once a week, either at their house or mine.

On one occasion, I invited both of them to go to a show with me. Mary refused, so Harry and I went on our own. Harry told me later that Mary was upset because he went without her. Harry and Mary have been together for seven years, which Harry admitted was the result of a "rebound" after his breakup with his ex-wife.

Harry and I naturally began doing things together. Each time we say goodnight, we give each other a peck on the lips. Our conversations are solely about his relationship with Mary. He says he can't break up with her because he still loves her.

Suddenly, Mary called to say she was leaving Harry, and that she hated his guts. I was supposed to go to their Christmas party, however, by this time, I was beginning to realize that I had feelings for Harry and that I was no longer impartial. I didn't go to the party.

Mary walked out on Harry. When she called to again ask for my advice, I said that if she does not want to be with him, she should leave as planned. She verbally attacked me with, "Oh, really? Well I will show you." That ended the relationship with Mary and me. There would be no more cozy dinners at each other's houses. I told Harry I could no longer be in the middle of things, because I was no longer impartial. I never admitted I cared about him. But I moved 90 miles away.

Harry continued to email me and I responded. Still, the conversation was always about him and Mary. Months later, on his way to a sporting event, Harry and I went to dinner. I listened to him talk about Mary, we ate dinner, had a few drinks, and laughed. But on this night, when he walked me to my car, he put his arms around me, and kissed me, not like we're friends.

I was confused. I emailed him to explain. He replied that I shouldn't read anything into it. I told him we needed to discuss it and I didn't want to do it through email. He called me and said he was just "using me." I told him to stuff it. He begged me not to let our friendship go. I cared for him and I liked the hugs and kisses so I agreed.

The next time we got together, he told me he didn't think of me as a "sexual partner," only as a friend. I tried to push myself on him, and forced him to put his arms around me and kiss me. Talk about a dead fish! But we kept on communicating after that. I continued whining about unrequited love, and he continued to ignore my advances.

Months later, we went dancing during which he looked deep into my eyes and held me tight. But at dinner, he had told me he was "not where I was, and he did not know if he ever would be."

At Christmas, he invited me to his annual Christmas Party, and Mary was there. We all acted as though nothing was up. Now he said that Mary does her thing and he does his. He said it was his house, not Mary's. Although I told him to kiss off, I gave in again. By this time, I felt deep love for the sucker. Now when we got together, he would kiss me, hold me, and tell me he wished I still lived next door. I asked him if he still felt that he loved Mary. He said he felt "responsible" for her. Please, Dr. Gilda, what is your take on this? Perplexed

Okay, you the reader have just read this sad scenario. Since I've been telling you that we can analyze our behaviors by reading our own writing, what is YOUR impression? More specifically, do you believe Perplexed is feeling worthy of the whole enchilada? Clearly, she's not, and I told her so.

Dear Perplexed,

I don't mind telling you that this situation stinks, along with your ridiculous behavior! You have allowed yourself to be "used," by Harry's own admission, and the amazing part is that even after you moved far away and stopped congregating with this dismal duo, you changed your mind repeatedly and kept returning for more abuse! Don't you believe you deserve more than being on hold IF Harry ever leaves Mary? The guy's abusive because he knows how you feel about him, yet he continues to tease you, and to use you as a therapist in his saga of "alleged" misery, and as a woman who adores him, unlike the woman he's living with.

I use the words, "alleged misery" because if he were miserable enough, he'd leave. Further, if you were a real therapist, you'd get paid for your advice without getting emotionally involved. On some level, do you think you're being "paid" anyway with this dude's attention? If so, his kind of attention is worse than no attention at all.

Your own behavior is childish. You tell Harry to "kiss off," and then you press him to "kiss on." You're playing as much of a game with him as Harry is playing with you. What's more, even if he were to leave Mary, would you ever, ever, ever trust him to be faithful to you? Seeing the way he's treating the woman he "allegedly loves," and talking horribly behind her back, do you really believe he would be different with you? And if so, he'd be in another rebound relationship, which could simply be his usual pattern!

Girl, you're living in Dreamland. Harry teases you with body language and a few kisses, and then withdraws his flirting. It's cat-and-mouse between the two of you, and, frankly, Mary's no better for asking your opinion about whether to leave Harry, and then attacking you for offering it. The two of them are on a collision course. But apparently, you're right in there with them.

Frankly, I don't know why you're bothering to ask me what you should do when it's clear that you're doing whatever you please, no matter how it's hurting you, and any possible chances for Harry and you to ever get together.

How can you be so desperate that you're willing to push yourself on a guy? Don't you know that's a big turn-off to any man? And to think you believe you "love the sucker," when he hasn't given you anything to go on!

Perplexed, it's time to change YOUR name to "Sucker," and see the light. I wonder if you're hanging on to the notion of Harry because you're scared of having a man all your own. Open your mouth and take a nibble of a whole enchilada. While waiting around for nothing to happen, you don't know what you're missing with someone else.
Dr. Gilda

The whole enchilada is out there for anyone willing to take a bite. Yet many people don't feel worthy of even a tiny nibble.

Dear Dr. Gilda,

I have befriended a man over the course of 6 years and I can't tell if he's interested in a short term, over-night, or permanent marital relationship. Upon our getting to know each other, he was exiting a 19-year marriage. We are both Christians and spend a great deal of time together. He invites me to movies, to his home for dinner, and even on trips. He has also given me gifts and cards. However, he has never approached me sexually, or shared his intentions. I wonder if he is afraid to approach me because of our religious beliefs, or because of pain from his divorce that he hasn't yet resolved. He is, no doubt, attracted to me.

This guy is self-employed, educated, and a good father, with custody of three daughters. I can't figure out what to do. I don't want to foil a good friendship, but I desire him. I flirt with him, and drop hints, but seemingly, I'm not getting through. I am 46 and divorced, with an 11-year-old son. I'm in college, I am employed, and I'm very confident. I know that he is not involved with another woman, because much of his free time is spent on the phone with me. Can you help me figure this out?
Margie

Dear Margie,

While you believe you are "very confident," why are you not confident enough to ask this man about his intentions? This is not a casual friendship that has lasted merely a few weeks or months. Presumably, as the friends you are, the two of you share intimate and personal confidences. After six years, you have a right to know whether this guy is in for the long haul, or whether he intends to keep you as a platonic friend, thereby depriving you of finding a suitable marital partner.

If you really believe you're worthy of more, take the risk and ask him what his take on the situation is. If he can't tell you by now, he may never be able to tell you. If he can tell you, six years is a long enough time to begin to move the relationship to a deeper level.

So instead of asking me about this guy's intentions, it's time to ask him. Believe you are worthy of asking this very vital question, and believe you are worthy of getting an honest response.

Gilda-Gram®
What you believe, you will achieve.

Girlfriend, the ball's now in your court! Pick it up, and aim for the basket.
Dr. Gilda

Unfortunately, too many people don't fathom that their own beliefs are at the heart of their issues. And they can't imagine they can achieve much at all.

Dear Dr. Gilda,

My boyfriend of almost 4 years (he's 24, and I'm

41

22) beats me, not all the time, but most of the time. It's usually when he's drunk. He hits me very hard, as though I'm a man. This is followed by curse words that put me down, making me feel like I am nobody. Worst of all is that we have a little girl, 2 years old, who sees a lot of this. I fear for her, not because he'll hurt her, because he loves his daughter, but when she gets older, she may think it's okay for a man to hit her. Everybody has told me to leave him. People have even given me phone numbers of women's shelters. But I love this guy deeply, and I made the decision not to go. I'm writing to you so you can help me help him with his problem. He's not the type to get help, but I'm going to find a way to make this work. No matter what, I am not leaving.
Dora

Dear Dora,

I need to understand your position better. This man beats you, curses you, and makes you feel like "nobody." Your two-year-old daughter watches much of this, but you're certain he wouldn't hurt her, because he loves her. Yet, you fear that she may grow up believing that it's okay for a man to hit her.

You say you "love" this guy and you refuse to budge from your house. Instead, you want my help to help him, although he's not the type to accept help from anyone. Now that you read these words back, what do you think is wrong with this picture?

For starters, anyone who beats anyone else, especially if she's smaller than he, is a coward. Cowards not only bully those who can't fight back, they

42

also wait until they can blame their disgusting behavior on a substance, such as alcohol, so they can deny responsibility for their actions. Your cowardly boyfriend beats you in full view of the daughter he allegedly loves.

Well, Dora, I'm an educator, and here's the low-down on how children learn. Although she's just two years old, she's old enough for the sight of dad beating mom to remain in her mind forever. This image will create the model for her to mirror in her love life later on. Even if you tell her that her daddy's behavior is not acceptable, she is watching you not only accept it, but remain in this unhealthy, demeaning, and disrespectful environment.

What's wrong, not with your boyfriend, but with YOU for being such a glutton for punishment? Be aware that while you're being beaten physically, your child is being beaten emotionally. Is that fair to this innocent little creature? Is this what you would define as a loving parent? It's bad enough that your man is damaging his daughter by letting her observe this violence. But you're doing no better by not protecting her from seeing it.

There's no question about what you must do next: take your child and run. It's no longer only for your preservation; now it's for the safety of your daughter. Get off the fantasy of trying to save this delinquent. He's not worthy of being saved, and you're not Mother Theresa, or his social worker. But your daughter is still young enough to have a chance. At

least, be a responsible parent and give it to her!
Dr. Gilda

People hang out with people like themselves because those are the folks they feel most comfortable with, and those are the people they THINK they most trust. On the other side of the coin, worthy partners attract other worthy partners.

So if you're involved in a relationship that is not serving you, DECIDE FIRMLY, *not* who your partner is, but who YOU are—and what you really and truly deserve! Yes, as I continue to repeat, everything begins with us. When you are SURE that you're worthy of total commitment and love, that's exactly what you will find—and in the right person!

CHAPTER 5
4 SECRETS OF WORTHY LOVE

Although no authors I know of have outlined the secrets of worthy love, these mysteries are occasionally hidden in the pages of lots of books. Believe it or not, one of these wise tombs is a children's book that's been around for over half a century, and has been translated into different languages throughout the world. It's called "The Little Prince." The reason it's been popular for so long is because its message is not just for kids. In fact, I believe it fully explains worthy love—if you read it with your heart.

As the story goes, The Little Prince lives on his own tiny planet inhabited by a sole flower and some caterpillars. The flower is a beautiful rose, and her perfume permeates the entire planet. She's got attitude—and The Little Prince can't seem to get enough of her. (Ladies, haven't we seen this theme before? The girl with attitude is most attractive to the man—because she truly believes in herself, and she's not afraid to show it.)

Unlike any creature he has ever met (there aren't

too many on his planet), this flower is not shy about asking for what she wants. The Little Prince never before heard anyone speak up for herself. The flower knows what she needs, and she's happy to communicate it. For example, without hesitation, she asked The Little Prince to protect her with a glass globe, to shield her from the cold and the caterpillars. The Little Prince happily consented—because what man doesn't enjoy comforting and providing for a female in whom he's interested?

Maybe The Little Prince felt limited by being on this tiny planet with no other men to talk to. Maybe he felt a need to hunt for adventure—which is common for most males. Whatever his motivation was, The Little Prince took off on a long expedition far away, to visit asteroids and other planets. He left the flower behind to fend for herself, although she now had that protection from the glass globe. But the flower was independent enough to make it alone, and she didn't whine about remaining on the planet solo.

On his journey, The Little Prince met many men. They spoke of things they thought were "matters of consequence." These were material things that answered the questions, "How expensive?" "How much?," "How many?," "How soon?" But The Little Prince noted that these men had never seen a star, smelled a flower, or loved anyone. He knew that although they talked of "matters of consequence," these men were missing things that were *really* of consequence. And thus he learned that the greatest "things" in life are not "things" at all, but feelings people share with one another.

On one of the planets to which he traveled, The Little Prince came upon 5,000 flowers in one garden that all resembled the very flower he liked on his own planet. He was amazed. Then he met a fox he wanted to befriend. The fox refused. He told The Little Prince that they could not play together until The Little Prince tamed him. When The Little Prince didn't understand the meaning of being "tamed," the fox explained that "to tame" means "to establish ties." The fox said that after they established ties, they would need each other, they'd be committed, and they'd be unique to one another, unlike any relationship they knew with anyone else. Wow!

The Little Prince asked the fox how he could tame him. The animal said that it takes time and patience. At first, the two of them would just sit and stare into each other's eyes. Day by day, they'd move closer until they felt a genuine bond. When that bond was tied, they'd both know the fox was tamed.

After the fox taught The Little Prince the meaning of commitment, the fox suggested The Little Prince compare his sole flower to the garden of 5,000 he had seen. The fox explained that the sole flower would be unique to The Little Prince because he had "tamed" it. Because it was *she* that he had watered, put under the glass globe, and protected from the cold and caterpillars. The fox wisely said that it was the time he had spent with her that made her special. The sole rose had become HIS rose.

With this lesson of what was really of consequence, The Little Prince returned to his tiny planet, where he could be reunited with his flower. He had learned from the fox that you become responsible for and committed to whomever you have developed ties with.

I don't think it's an accident that I discovered these secrets hidden in the pages of "The Little Prince," while I was naming one of the books I wrote, "Don't Bet on the Prince!"

For sure, most males have been raised as princes of one kind or another. Unlike the flower, many women are reluctant to speak their mind and ask for what they need. They hold their tongues because they're afraid to rock the relationship boat. Ultimately, they fear they'll frighten away the man.

Containing your true feelings ruins a relationship. Men find that these shutdown women they initially liked during their first encounter, have now become boringly agreeable, and hardly the challenging and intriguing people they thought they had found.

Gilda-Gram®
When people become bored in a relationship, they leave.

The Little Prince's flower was different from the

women who don't feel worthy enough to speak their mind. She spoke up and asked for help when she needed it. And when The Little Prince decided to go on his adventure without her, she didn't plead with him to stay home and babysit her. She didn't even cry when he left. She accepted his desire to travel the world as part of whom he was and what he needed to do. She independently remained on her planet doing her own thing.

When The Little Prince was ready, he returned to her. But when he did, the insight he had gained from his travels caused him to appreciate her worth all the more.

"The Little Prince" teaches us 4 Secrets of Worthy Love. (And I really mean *worthy*!) They are:

1) <u>Consider Yourself Unique.</u>

The flower was so confident about her uniqueness, she didn't feel abandoned when The Little Prince chose to pursue his adventures.

List two of your most wonderful traits. Focus on these as you follow your day's agenda. Each time you greet someone, think of these traits. Allow them to guide you as you carry yourself with confidence and grace.

Notice that people respond to you with the same elegance you present to them. Note how this exercise applies the adage, "What goes around comes around."

2) <u>Create Your Own Excitement.</u>

The little flower was happy to remain on her tiny planet, with or without The Little Prince. No one makes you happy. No one gives you a better life. You are totally responsible for your own contentment and excitement. And when you display your personal excitement about life, you will attract exciting and committed partners.

Dear Dr. Gilda,

I had a platonic male friend for 25 years. Last year, we began to see each other romantically. While I was really into him, I felt that he did not feel the same way, so I broke it off. He waited a while, and we started up together again. We still haven't become a committed couple.

He feels that things should just flow, to see where we end up. I hate this approach. Although I'm crazy about him, I stopped seeing him again. Am I asking too much to set boundaries in this relationship? Should I just go with the "flow," not knowing what to expect? Is he handing me some line that men use when they are not sure they want a commitment?
Carla

Dear Carla,

Even though you're not wearing a ring, what's wrong with just enjoying the journey? Girl, you waited 25 years to get to this point. So now, what's your rush?

Men are often slower than women to decide they want to settle down. There are differences in our gender makeup.

Gilda-Gram®
Men fear that women are invasive, while women fear that men are evasive.

It's obvious that there's deep emotion between the two of you. Otherwise, this guy would not keep returning. Give him the time he seems to need without trying to control him. Let him conclude by himself that you are the one. Meanwhile, get a separate life! Start scheduling things you love to do, and pursue them with gusto. This way, you won't be worrying more about the relationship than you are about satisfying your personal desires. That, in itself, will make you more alluring, and more patient, as well!
Dr. Gilda

Worthy partners are interesting partners. InterestING partners are interestED partners. Interested partners are very attractive, and they're the ones that titillate their mates to come back for more.

3) Understand Your Partner's Needs.

The flower recognized The Little Prince's need to travel to become wiser. She was not too proud or insecure to ask him to place the glass globe over her to protect her from the cold while he was gone. And she never tried to stand in his way, or even to talk him out of it, when he announced that he was departing.

Dear Dr. Gilda,

I am a 35-year old woman with 2 girls, 11 and 15. My husband and I have been married for 12 years. He left us 6 months ago, because he said he was unhappy. I didn't think I was a bad wife. But it was hard for me to be a working mother and a housewife at the same time. I thought the man of the house was supposed to help out. When my man didn't, I told him to pack his bags and move in with his mother, hoping it would get him to help.

For the last three years, it did make him start helping around the house. Well, the last time I told him to pack up, he said he couldn't take it anymore, and he left for good. He says he's not in love with me, but he will always love me. He says that being around me is like being with a friend. He's seeing someone now. I need help to make this marriage work. Please help me! Rebecca

Dear Rebecca,

Sometime during your marriage, you stopped being your guy's wife, in exchange for becoming his shrew! Your marriage became a sham in that all you did was hassle him about helping you. What happened to love, respect, and devotion? When he didn't follow your directives, you tried to manipulate him by telling him to leave.

At first, your manipulations worked, and he

continued to return home. But after a while, as is always the case, your plotting got old, and he fell into the arms of someone who apparently wanted him as more than just a help-mate around the house.

Understand what men need. They need their women to appreciate them, support them, and make them feel worthy. You missed the boat. Now you ask for "help to make this marriage work." I can't and won't help you manipulate him back into your arms. Accept the fact that your marriage is over. The best you can do is to understand where you went wrong, learn that lesson well, and move on. Hopefully, the next guy with whom you connect will feel that you value him for more than just what he can do for you.
Dr. Gilda

4) To Have a Worthy Partner, Be a Worthy Partner.

The flower withstood the harsh winter, while The Little Prince learned the true meaning of love. Upon his return, because of his vast experiences, he was more capable of giving to the flower. This Secret applies the expression, "What you give out, you get back."

Dear Dr. Gilda,

Jim and I have been together for 2 years. A few months back, we were fighting all the time. We could barely talk to each other. I thought he was insanely jealous, and he thought I was a bitch. I made the decision to move out.

Soon, I ran into my previous boyfriend who had burned me badly. I went out with him because I wanted closure in knowing what I did that made him cheat on me during a time when I needed him most. Jim found out that I stayed with this guy for most of a weekend. We did not have sex, but after that, he kept calling, and it drove Jim nuts. "Closure" for Jim meant one last romp in the hay. He couldn't understand that it didn't mean the same for me.

Then suddenly, I discovered I was pregnant. It was overwhelming, to say the least. I was on the pill and hadn't planned to have a baby at this stage of my life. I told Jim and he was excited, thinking a baby would make our problems disappear. I got cold feet and told him I needed space. The space I was talking about was a couple of days, maybe a couple of weeks. He took it to mean that we were done. His pride wouldn't allow him to wait.

One day, I called to tell him that I didn't like our space and that I loved him, although I needed to work out some issues on my own. During the conversation, he told me he had met someone else, and it was over between us. I couldn't believe it.

After a couple of weeks, we talked again. He said he still loved me, and that he got himself into a situation, and now he didn't want to hurt his new woman. Basically, since then, he has continued to date her and me. He says that I hurt him and that until he's ready to give us a chance again, he probably will continue to date her. I don't understand.

We've talked about going to counseling. We both want the same things. He still gets upset if he hears that a guy has asked me out or even calls. We both love each other, and I think the fact that we are having a child is important. I know a child is not a reason to stay together and that isn't the case. I haven't dated anyone since we split.

Jim is supportive of the baby and me. We've done the doctor visits and baby shopping together. He's going to be there for the birth, and he plans to stay at my house for a while after the baby is born. It makes the situation with the other woman very hard. What do you suggest I do?
Alicia

Dear Alicia,

You've gotten yourself, and now your unborn child, into a bind. You say Jim is insanely jealous, yet you allowed him to find out that you sought "closure" with your ex. And the definition of "closure" differs between the two of you. I'm afraid that, like Jim, I don't understand why "closure" for you meant investing in a whole weekend, when all you wanted was to discover the information of why he cheated on you. You then let Jim know that this guy is now difficult to get rid of. It appears that if Jim is jealous to begin with, you're flaming the fires, and enjoying his jealousy as a way to prove he still cares. No wonder the two of you fight incessantly!

It's not the English language that seems to stump you. You never explained specifically what you meant by both "closure" and "space." So Jim just interpreted them as "rejection" and "termination," as he continued to get his feelings pummeled.

Interestingly, as soon as Jim seemed excited about having a baby, you chose to distance yourself from him for an unspecified length of time. You figured you'd get "a couple of days" or "a couple of weeks" to breathe on your own. But he interpreted these words to mean "forever." Although not the healthiest of reactions, Jim then chose to get on with his life with another woman. You can't blame him for wanting to protect himself from you. How much back-and-forth teasing should someone endure?

I don't doubt that, pregnant or not, your continued taunting of him with closeness and then distance wore him down. So I'd have to agree that Jim's description of you as a "bitch" may rightfully be deserved.

You still have your fangs into this guy, and he's dumb enough to leave them in his back. Surely, he's financially and emotionally responsible for helping to raise this baby, and he's apparently glad to take on this task—which says a great deal about his ethical character. But he's now in protective mode, arming himself against any more pain. And that's why he's not about to let his other woman go. Actually, I feel sorry for her, because no one should ever get involved with someone like Jim, who's in a state of unresolved transition.

As it stands, he's neither with her, nor is he with you. He is terribly confused. And so are you. It's really pitiful that an innocent baby has to appear in this mix that involves so much confusion and pain.

At this time, provide all the support you can for this harmless little being. As for your own future, you must first learn to become a worthy partner, if ever you want to hold on to a good guy.
Dr. Gilda

Gilda-Gram®
To have a worthy partner, BE a worthy partner. To be a worthy partner, BELIEVE that you are worthy yourself.

***

Benefit from
Dr. Gilda's personal Advice & Coaching
www.DrGilda.com

***

Dr. Gilda's Relationship Series
--8 Steps to a Sizzling Marriage
--8 Tips to Understand the Opposite Sex

--10 Questions Single Women Should Never Ask
& 10 They Should
--10 Signs of a Cheater-to-Be

Dr. Gilda's Self-Worth Series
-- "I'm Worth Loving! Here's Why."
-- "Ask for What You Want—AND GET IT!
-- "How to Be a Worry-Free Woman"

Dr. Gilda's Fidelity Series
--Why Your Cheater Keeps Cheating—And You're
Still There!
--How to Cope with the Cheater You Love—and WIN
--99 Prescriptions for Fidelity: *Your Rx for Trust*

ALSO
--Don't Bet on the Prince! *How to Have the Man You
Want by Betting on Yourself*
--Don't Lie on Your Back for a Guy Who Doesn't
Have Yours

***

Dr. Gilda Carle (Ph.D.) is an internationally
known media personality and relationship expert. She
has authored 15 books, including "Don't Bet on the
Prince!" (a test question on "Jeopardy!"), "Teen Talk
with Dr. Gilda," "He's Not All That!," "How to WIN
When Your Mate Cheats" (winner of The London Book
Festival literary award), "99 Prescriptions for Fidelity,"
and more. She also wrote the weekly "30-Second
Therapist" column for the Today Show, and the "Ask

Dr. Gilda" advice columnist for Match.com.

On TV, Dr. Gilda was the regular therapist for the Sally Jessy Raphael show, the "Love Doc" for MTV Online, and the TV host of "The Dr. Gilda Show" pilot for Twentieth Century Fox. In addition, she was the therapist in HBO's Emmy Award winner, "Telling Nicholas," featured on Oprah, where she guided a family to tell their 7-year-old that his mom died in the World Trade Center bombing.

In academia and the corporate sector, she has been a management consultant, Professor Emerita, motivational speaker, and product spokesperson.

As President of Country Cures, Inc., a non-profit 501(c)(3) educational charity organization, she is the "Country Music Doctor." As such, the organization uniquely uses country music to provide education and training for transitioning veterans and their families. If you, or someone you know, can benefit from this help, please visit **www.CountryCures.org**.

————————

Reach Dr. Gilda at
www.DrGilda.com
or
www.CountryCures.org

www.ingramcontent.com/pod-product-compliance
Lightning Source LLC
Chambersburg PA
CBHW071638040426
42452CB00009B/1682